THE
POWER
OF
BELIEF

DERRICK PICKETT

THE CREDIT GURU

TABLE OF CONTENTS

BET ON YOU

INVICTUS
William Ernest Henley

Out of the night that covers me,
Black as the pit from pole to pole,
I thank whatever gods may be
For my unconquerable soul.

In the fell clutch of circumstance
I have not winced nor cried aloud.
Under the bludgeonings of chance
My head is bloody, but unbowed.

Beyond this place of wrath and tears
Looms but the Horror of the shade,
And yet the menace of the years
Finds and shall find me unafraid.

It matters not how strait the gate,
How charged with punishments the scroll,
I am the master of my fate,
I am the captain of my soul.

DEDICATION

This book is dedicated to my spiritual father, mentor, and brother, the late Antonio (Tony) Hurt.

I wrote my first book three years ago without him knowing, and he was very upset at me because I didn't tell him. It was a surprise that ended up surprising me. I didn't understand at the time why he was so mad, but later I got it.

He didn't want me to publish a book just to say I published a book. He wanted me to publish a book that represented my brand. Because of him, I have been able to help so many others. We shared countless conversations and heartfelt moments that most people won't ever understand.

It's rare in life when a person says they can meet themselves in another person. When I really met Tony Hurt, I met a man who was full of greatness. So many times when I thought I was helping him, he was really helping me. He helped me find the person I really was and his memory pushes me to pursue the greatness that is within me. He pushed me to write four more books, and I'm still counting the books that I still must write. He taught me the 'power of me' and ignited my ability to believe in myself. Most people don't really know how it is to meet a man at his highest high and his lowest low and still get treated the same. Tony has taught me how to give and realize what faith and humanity really is all about. I remember a few prayers that were pivotal in my life, and one of them was once when he was discouraged and didn't want to write anymore. I prayed that night, "Lord, let him keep writing." For whatever reason, I knew that it wasn't time for him to quit, and I now know that his quitting would have been detrimental to my success. There are times when our prayers for others are actually our prayers for ourselves.

My prayers were answered, and he is the reason I truly wanted to write a book because I saw him do it so easily. I am grateful that I met him, and I am grateful that we were friends. Most of all, I am grateful he saw the best in me and invested in me when I wouldn't invest in myself. He was definitely a man of God, and I know he was sent as an angel in my life. My life will never be the same, and yours won't be either because he pushed me to be a better me to help you.

INTRODUCTION

When you first meet me, you may find that I'm a little shy and reserved, but there is a depth of character within me that goes unnoticed once I begin to open my mouth.

I love to joke and laugh and have fun. I can spin any situation around and bring out joy, laughter, and hope. I'm the type of guy that hates to rest in depression, doubt, or death. I believe in the possibilities of life through the power of God.

Somewhere in life something happened to me. I began to believe in the power of God over my life despite my failures and flaws. I became captivated by success and would no longer allow the allure of failure to drag me into a web that would deceive me.

I have made some mistakes in life, and I continue to make them daily. However, I now know that the power of faith should bring you into a place where you believe in yourself. YOU are your greatest asset, and you attract greatness to you when you begin to hone in on your skills through the power of your belief.

I wrote this book with you in mind, knowing that there is so much in store for you that you can't even imagine. If you are willing to BET ON YOU, you will find that things will begin to change in your life. Now that you have bet on everyone else, it's time to believe in the power resting within you.

BET ON YOU. BELIEVE IN YOU. TRUST IN YOU.
Derrick Anthony Pickett

BECOME A NURSE

January 11, 1985.
I remember this day just like it was yesterday. In fact, it was.

I sat as a little boy at Pleasant Baptist Church and saw the man I wanted to be.

I saw this older man, Rev. Hawk, preach the word of God and set souls on fire. That was the day I knew I wanted to be a pastor/leader/preacher.

I hung around the church and joined the choir, only to be quickly discouraged by a man who told me that being a pastor wasn't a bed of roses because you would have to take care of too many people and the phone would never stop ringing.

...August 2018, while I was moving my daughter into college, I got a phone call from a guy named Bill Williams.

Bill is a hard worker, a nurse, who worked countless hours. As a matter of fact, he was referred by a client when he was taking personal care of the client's daddy. That day he told me that he wanted to get a house which his daddy built that was up for sale. The house was a modest house that he could easily afford, but he had challenging credit holding him back.

I told him to send me over his information, and after carefully looking at it, I told him I could do it. We met, I talked to him, and we began the process. Then, less than 30 days later his score was good enough to qualify. He was surprised, and he even took me to lunch to thank me.

One of the things I often realize is that so many of my clients have been hurt by people before. I must slow down and give them hope, but also follow-through with them as partners-in-hope. Credit restoration and strategizing for their next move isn't the hard part about what I do; it's nursing the people back to belief. It's not easy to believe when you are walking in the midst of brokenness, and I get the opportunity to help people even as I am restored from the brokenness that I have experienced in my life.

On November 21, 2018, Bill called to tell me that he had closed on his house, after only three months of working with me. I was so happy because I felt like I was able to help a nurse who had helped so many people feel better about himself and his future. I felt better because I was given the opportunity to become a nurse to a nurse. I nursed the believe back in him. Now he has the house that his daddy built, and he is proud to say that he is a homeowner.

As a point of reference, Mark 9:23-24 is one of my favorite passages of scripture. It's a place where a man had to allow the possibilities of his future to meet his unbelief. Although Jesus shared that all things were possible to those who believed, this man with a sick child had to encounter his own unbelief in order to get to the healing of his child.

We all have a level of unbelief that is resting within us, and we don't encounter it until we are confronted with the true possibilities of change. That scripture continues to touch me because most people have more unbelief than they do belief.

Life is tricky, and it can get the best of you. No matter how you work to move forward, you can find yourself feeling lost and hopeless, wondering if there will ever be a break in store for you.

I soon realized that God sent a nurse on my path for me to nurse back to spiritual and financial freedom through assisting him to get the house that his daddy built. This example of faith caused me to realize that I pastor people on many levels by bringing them hope, deliverance, and restoration. The fire that I wanted back as a child is now flowing through me as I give my clients the personal care that is needed for the next phase of their lives.

Never forget the power and passion that is lying dormant in your soul. Perhaps there are things within you that are being nursed back to health as you nurse those around you in their change. The day Bill called me, I became a nurse, a pastor, a leader, a friend. Bill is in his home, and I rejoice with him.

Bet on you. Believe in you. Trust in you.

BECOME A BARBER

If anyone knows me, they know I love family, and I love helping people. In fact, my love for my family and people has proven to be a help and a hindrance in my life.

…I was headed to our yearly family reunion in 2016, which was in Atlanta.

I have always been a sort of jack of all trades and never a man focusing on one thing. This, too, has been an asset but also causes a depreciation in my value at times.

In July 2016, I got a call when I was inside a store from a young man who owned a barbershop. I was in the store buying some things from the many coupons that I had clipped.

He called me and told me he heard I was good at credit repair, and he needed my help. It's amazing how my true call came forth while I was amid doing something that would not bring me the wealth or satisfaction that I wanted in life. I now know many great couponers and understand the value of saving a dollar, but I also understand the power of receiving your true call while doing what you think you are called to do.

Needless to say, I finished shopping and went to meet him. He had been barbering for many years and wanted to buy the building that he was renting. I knew it was an easy task because he only had one derogatory item on his credit.

It was a big thing that needed to be done, but I knew how to do it. After I talked to him, he told me how he was feeling after countless attempts to fix his credit. So many people had failed him, and I knew I had to solve his problem. Not to mention I was new to credit repair and I was still proving myself, he would prove to be one of the biggest paying clients that I had ever had.

…This is a very good barber who stands for hours mastering his craft. He told me that he was in the shop by himself, often 12 hours at a time taking care of his clients. Barbering is a tiring job, not just because you stand on your feet for hours, but because all the stories you must listen to that rest in your spirit for years after one haircut. We pay our barbers and beauticians a small fee for amazing service, but we leave so much of us in them as they pour out so much of themselves into us.

I have always honored the spirit of my barbers because the humanity that rests in them is beyond the minor conversations and the awesome look that they bestow upon me. Beyond making me look and feel good, I have found that they often serve with excellence without even getting a small tip.

…After talking to him that day, I went to my family reunion and saw my little sister who was into couponing as well. That day she asked me for some coupons, and I went in my trunk and gave them all to her. That day I retired from couponing and made a decision for my life. God told me, "you can't make millions chasing pennies."

That day, my client, Tony, taught me a lesson about doing what you love with all your heart, and the money will chase you.

He made me realize that I had a higher calling as a credit consultant, and I became a licensed barber in the spirit. As I listened to his story and helped him feel better, look better, and attain his goals and dreams, I soon realized that I must continue to master my craft by standing on my feet for hours in order to honor my clients.

A week later his problem was solved with his credit. Two months later, I helped him get all the funds for the building, so he could buy it. I was happy that I met him because he made me realize that I had the power to change lives if I made the sacrifices needed for my clients. Sometimes, it takes stories from others to make us realize what we have in us.

LIFE'S TRANSITIONS

You may have heard that there are different chapters to your life but missed the point as a result of the fast pace that you were living.

At one point in my life, I was a guy who went around to beauty salons and barber shops selling plastic business cards. That was when I learned what it felt like to be a traveling salesman. I met a lot of people, and I loved that industry because of the creative energy, servitude, and gratitude that flows at unexpected times.

I retired from selling business cards after I realized I was good at credit restoration. This was not an easy transition because I was leaving something that I loved and had become comfortable with to enter a place where I had to listen and learn on a new level. So often in life, people always want you to be who you used to be. It's easy to revert to your old ways and the things that come easy to you, but you must be diligent in knowing that there are painful transitions that you must make in life.

Even though most of us start in kindergarten and eventually graduate out of the 12th grade, we find ourselves around people who forget about life's transitions. In fact, we forget about life's transitions and hold on to things that we should be letting go of. You must be careful and not allow yourself or others to keep you in a position or place just because you became good at it. The things that you were good at can stop you from being great at the things that force you to be better.

I did business cards for so long that some of my clients won't let others sell them business cards. I soon realized that my clients were so familiar with the old that they only wanted that part of me. At this juncture, I must remind myself that I am not who I used to be while introducing them to the new me.

…In February 2018, I got a call from an old client who had just recently relocated their salon and wanted some business cards. As a courtesy and maybe to be a little nosey, I went out to see them, but when I was there, I told them that I was in the business of changing lives by restoring credit. I told her that I didn't like doing business cards anymore, but I could help her with her credit. We talked briefly and months passed only to later find that this lady was caught in a credit restoration program that had been dragging her for over a year. I listened to her pain only to realize that people will question how good you are at your job that it will make you question yourself. She even tried to get me to team up with the person who had been working on her credit.

Needless to say, that person didn't know more than me. After a few months past, she finally let me start restoring her credit and her life.

As a result of life's traumas and the lack of skill that they have experienced at the hands of others, most of my clients don't believe that their credit can be restored. After years of paying cash and surviving with bad credit, most people learn how to survive rather than truly believe for their life transitions. This lady was no different, so I would check her credit weekly and within a month her file was clean. She couldn't even believe it was done.

It took me over a month to get her to slow down and look at her credit. Three months later, I helped her build her credit so she could get the funding needed to finance and grow her business. The beauty of what I do rests in the fact that I can help people grow, dream, and believe in the possibilities that are in store for them. Through the power of transition, I have been transformed from the guy who does cards to the guy who specializes in credit restoration and financial freedom.

It's truly a good feeling to help people see what they have inside of them is something that's more beautiful than what's on the outside, but you must bet on you, trust in you, and believe in you, even when you struggle with life's transitions.

CONDITIONS CHANGE

There are some stories in life that forever stay in your heart.

I'll never forget that at one of the lowest points in my life God let me meet this strong guy by the name of Popeye.

That was his nickname, but he told me something that made me realize why they call him Popeye. If you don't know, Popeye is a cartoon character that got strength after he ate his spinach. I met a real-life Popeye who had been through some things in life that most people would have died from.

Popeye and I were having a group discussion with some guys, and we saw a picture in a book of a house that was dirty and in bad shape. A young guy probably in his 20's made the statement when he saw the picture, "I could never live like that!" My friend, Popeye, quickly stopped the young man by saying, "don't ever day that!" He responded, "those are conditions, and conditions can change." He said, "just like it can be cold one day and hot the next, so can your life change."

That day forever changed my mindset about any conditions I had in my life that weren't good.

Five years later, I had the chance to change the conditions in my friend's life. He spoke words that forever changed my life, and I was glad to return the favor. Popeye called me and told me he wanted to start a business, and he needed some help. I was so happy to know that I could give back into someone who gave me so much and didn't even know it. So, I worked on his credit and within a few months his condition changed, and he was a business owner of a trucking company.

After getting his truck, Popeye had this amazing smile on his face that spoke volumes to my soul. He turned to me and said, "Now, I don't have to worry about selling drugs anymore, I am a business owner, and I didn't have to sell drugs to do it." It was at that very moment that I received another confirmation that I was doing what I was called and created to do: help change the lives of others.

You or someone you know may be living through some unfavorable conditions right now, but keep hope, faith, and belief at the forefront of your mind and always remember that your conditions can change.

PAY ATTENTION TO THE SIGNS IN THE ROAD

I'm sure most of you have heard the biblical story of Jonah in the belly of the whale. If you haven't read that story, you may need to read it.

I found myself being Jonah at one point in my life. I was in a dark place and no one could save me no matter how much money they had. In your darkest moments, that's when you see the light in life. This light may not be as bright as you think it should be, but it's the light of hope that shines forth amid darkness.

Well, I found myself in a strange place that made me get to know new people and learn new things. Some would call it hell, but I just say it was a hold-over station. On my journey in the belly of the whale, I was blessed to meet this older man, kind of like the guy on the movie the Green Mile that was played by Michael Clarke Duncan.

He was a big man with few words, but they were very powerful. This man was like a Neanderthal, a big guy but a gentle giant. This man named Jeremiah was a prophet and didn't even know it. He was such a brilliant man, but people were afraid of him because of his size. He battled some type of mental disorder or depression because he was on medication, and he slept most of the day. I didn't understand why he slept so much until later after we parted ways.

We only talked a few times, but the few times we talked were life changing. He told me how he was tricked into his current situation because he was trying to survive in life. He was facing a lot of time for a crime that he was set up in. I listened closely to his pain because he made me realize my problems were minor compared to his. We had several unique conversations, but one stood out more than others.

He told me about how he got where he was but, he gave me a life changing nugget: "pay attention to the signs in the road."

It went over my head at that moment because I was taking it all in.

Two years later, I ran into my partner who I was looking and praying for, Tony Hurt.

I told him those words, and he explained the meaning. So many times in life, the signs are right in front of us, but we must pay attention to them. We often get the warnings before things happen, and it's our job to pay attention. I am thankful for Mr. Jeremiah because he taught me how to slow down and pay attention to everything around me. He was a prophet and an angel at the same time. I pay attention to the signs that I receive daily, and I now know that people matter more than their pain or their problems. I learned in the belly of the whale that you can learn from anyone if you are willing to look beyond what you see to hear what they have to say. Mr. Jeremiah taught me a valuable tool in life that has carried me from that day forward.

Pay attention to the signs in the road.

TODAY PAYS FOR TOMORROW

It's a known fact that for corn and many other plants and vegetables to grow you must plant the seeds in dirt.

Dirt is an element in this world that we often don't like because it's seen as nasty. After countless dirty situations, I have learned to love dirt and its power. I found myself buried deep under dirt in some bad situations where I had the chance to talk to some other powerful seeds that were buried with me.

Most people ask me how I got into credit, and I vaguely tell them I stumbled upon it. The truth is I was hurt bad by someone who was supposedly cleaning my credit. I gave them a lot of money and referred them to a lot of people, but they lied to me and treated me like a dog. After being disappointed by this person who I put all my trust in, I decided to learn on my own.

I was blessed to sit at the feet of this wise guy who was a pilot that whispered in my ear one day while we were both underground in the dirt. He told me that credit was a good business, and I could make a lot of money in the business.

He was a seasoned man who had traveled the world and told me that credit was one of the most powerful things on this earth. So, I ordered some credit books and started reading. I read through them briefly, but I still didn't take it seriously.

A few years later I met a man who became my best friend and mentor. He was a guy who I met that taught me you can't judge a book by the cover. His name is Rio, and he was a guy who had a job of cleaning up bathrooms that most people considered dirty, but he did it with pride.

We had a brief conversation about credit one day and before you knew it, he had convinced me to pick back up credit restoration as a business. He told me about a friend of his that did credit and was very successful at it. He inspired me to pursue the great business full-time. He even gave me a book that forever changed my life.

Sometimes in life God will have you cross paths with people who have been where you want to go. I had a low moment, and it seemed like everyone was passing me, but he told me a timeless word when he said, "today pays for tomorrow." The light bulb went off in my head, and it helped me. He showed me that what I worked on today would help my tomorrow. So, he was the reason I started studying credit everyday by reading books and doing credit for free when I first got started. He taught me that if we work hard enough today, tomorrow would be better.

IT'S INSIDE OF YOU

I'm sure you have seen the classic movie, The Wizard of Oz.

I remember watching the movie but never thought I would have to live it. The movie is about 4 characters, the scare crow, tin man, the lion, and Dorothy. They felt like they were missing something in their life, so they wanted to see the wizard to get it. They took on a journey that made them meet themselves.

I was probably all those characters in the movie, and I am still on a journey of self-discovery. You see: all my life, I would look to others for something that was inside me. I forgot about the great man I was because I was always looking at others. I can't count all the money I spent going to seminars, videotapes, monthly memberships, and buying books I never read. I was a victim of analysis paralysis. I would over think things and not make any decisions, while asking others their opinions so I could make my decisions. I have studied so much information that at times it's hard to process it all.

In early 2018, I had the chance to be in a mastermind group of great men. It was very expensive to be in the group that was invitation only. After going one time, I realized that all I paid for was a membership to listen to a bunch of men who didn't feel like they were worthy of believing in themselves. I was one of them. I was paying someone else to find out that what I was looking for was already inside of me.

They told their stories, but deep down inside I know they just wanted to be validated. God has a way of sending you to you to find you. Even though I was not like them, I was just like them. Needless to say, I saw the wizard of Oz that day, and he told me that I had it in me.

If you don't think you are good enough, you need to know that you are more than enough. I want to save you a lot of money, pain, and years on waiting for someone to validate you. You have what it takes to make it, and don't be afraid to make mistakes. You have a unique gift that I know will change the world if only you believe.

I SURVIVED

When you have been at a low place in your life, you can think that you are weak, but you are stronger.

Many years ago, I met a man by the name of Michael Anthony. I remember when he was selling clothes out his trunk, and I was a client of his. He bought business cards from me for years, and I bought clothes from him.

I used to go talk to him when he had a store on a busy highway. His fifty dollars used to save my life at times when I was at my lowest, with no money at all.

We became good friends along the way, and I began to think of him as a mentor, only to find that he thought of me as a mentor as well. When you have a deep friendship and bond with someone, you will find that they are teaching you just as you are teaching them.

No matter how much I told him that I retired from making business cards, he would make me print some for him. He has this way about him that forces me to do what he asks me to do. He's just that kind of friend.

The last set of cards I printed for him made me stronger. He had been at a low place in his life, and he told me to add the words on his business cards "I SURVIVED." Those were only two words, but they were yet so powerful. I SURVIVED.

He made me realize that no matter where I may be in life that I am in a good place because I SURVIVED. He tells me all the time that he loves me and that I am his best friend. We don't talk that much, but when we get together we can always talk about how we survived when everyone left us. I quickly remind him that "it was painful, but necessary."

So often, we think we need people later to only realize that we are survivors and that whatever was missing brought out the best in us. When you look back over your life, look at everything you have survived, and when you think about the things that you are going through, remember that you have already survived.

A MADE-UP MIND

I believe everyone who has a big family of any sort has a favorite uncle or aunt.

I was blessed to have a big family, and my favorite uncle was my Uncle Bean. He was an old-school man who took care of his family. He had the spirit of the hustler and that was the man I wanted to be like.

He lived in the big city of New York. He was a hard worker who stayed in the projects for 40 years. He would come down to my hometown of Hawkinsville during the summer, and he would reach into his pocket and hand me some money. That twenty dollars that he would give me was like a thousand because I had a desire to always get money. He was instrumental in my mentality to never be broke.

When I was at my lowest point in life and felt like I had let him down, he spoke great words that lifted my spirit. On a brief phone conversation, which would be my last time talking to him, I said, "'Unck', I feel bad for what I've done." He quickly stopped me and said, "Nephew, don't feel bad. You were just trying to get some money. Many great men have done the same thing."

It wasn't that he was justifying my actions, but he refused to allow me to be defeated by the bad decisions that I had made. He told me that I just had to make up my mind I wasn't going to do it again and move on.

I did exactly that. I made up my mind, and I didn't do it again. My uncle passed shortly after that, but those words made him live in me forever. The truth is we all make mistakes, but it's up to us to change our mind about the mistakes and decide to do better. The mindset of a person determines everything. Once you make up your mind to do better, be better, and receive better, you will soon find the power of a made-up mind.

FORGIVE YOURSELF

It's a fact that we are often much harder on ourselves than we are on everyone else. Even if we are hard on others, it's really a reflection of how we feel about ourselves. There is no way that you can love yourself, and beat up on others, and there is no way that you can beat up on yourself if you truly love yourself.

I have been a victim of being hard on myself for years. Oftentimes, we harbor the past in our souls so much that we can't hardly move ahead. No matter how bad the mistake may be, it is still wise to let it go. You can't live a life of forward movement if you are not willing to let go of the things that hold you back.

It's a known fact that a lot of great things have been made from mistakes. Great recipes, great cars, great movies, and most of all, great people, have been made as a result of mistakes and bad decisions.

One of the major blocks that I deal with in the credit business is that most people can't get over their mistakes. They spend so much time talking about what went wrong that they can't focus on what the next move is. I have had to forgive myself so many times because I know that it's all part of the process. Even in the places where I struggle with forgiveness, I continue to reflect on the power of self-love over hatred and defeat.

This chapter is probably one of the most important chapters I wrote because I know a lot of my clients and readers have something that's holding them back from believing that they are greater than their current situation. You, my friend, are a winner, and please don't let one mistake define your whole life. Never think that you can't come back from the dark places and low points in your life. I am a living witness that there is a return after the fall, so forgive and love yourself.

THIS IS WHAT I DO

Most people don't have the pleasure of enjoying what they do, or perhaps they have not submitted to what they do to learn how to enjoy and receive the pleasure of doing what they have been called to do.

It all started like the movie, The Karate Kid. I was a young man who was bullied by the credit system and an old veteran came along and showed me how to win the credit fight.

I have had a lot of credit reports come across my desk that have the word "DELETED" on them. It brings me pure joy to know I have the ability to change someone's life through credit restoration, increasing their scores through tradelines, and assisting them in acquiring the funding needed to move forward.

One of the most heartbreaking stories I ever ran across was a young single mother who had worked hard all her life to maintain good credit called me crying like she had lost her child. I quickly asked her what was wrong, and she replied that she had consigned on a car for her child, and the child was late on their payment. I never knew credit could be so painful. I was determined to help solve the problem. One month later, the late payment was updated as current and her problem was solved.

At that point, I knew I had a higher calling to help millions of people get their life back in order, one person at a time. At times, it can be overwhelming. Like a surgeon after a long surgery, I see my clients in the recovery room being made healthy and whole again.

THE POWER OF TWO

I was told a long time ago that if you want to make God laugh, then tell him your plans.

I'm sure God is laughing at me every day because my plans just don't turn out how I plan. You would think that I would stop planning so much and just sit back and listen to the voice of God, but I'm working on that.

I had plans to have a big printing company like Kinkos, but I turned out being a guy who sold high end plastic business cards to barbers and stylist mostly.

I've traveled all over the country for over fifteen years selling plastic business cards at trade shows and going inside barber shops and beauty salons. I thought I was going to being doing that forever, but my life changed like the weather. The good thing about being an entrepreneur is that you build relationships that last forever. In fact, my work is more in the line of a consultant because people share so much with me about their lives that is beyond credit.

I had the opportunity to meet a young lady many years ago who bought a lot of cards from me when I was a young man trying to make it. She eventually inspired me to publish a magazine that I never saw coming. As time progressed, I eventually left the plastic card business and transitioned into the credit business. It was scary at first, but I had to leave because I knew I had to grow. This young lady was one of my first credit clients as a matter of fact. She was also at a transitional stage in her life and wanted to go into real estate.

She had been in the beauty industry for over twenty years but wanted to help people in another way.

After many failed tests and tears, she finally passed her real estate exam with excellence. If you know like I know, starting something new can be a challenge. She set out on the journey and began doing home buying seminars. I realized I was good at credit, but I still needed help with the resources to help my clients find their dream home. I had a couple who were at their wits end after I fixed their credit, so I passed the baton to my friend, and she walked them through the process.

It was a first for both of us. It was my first client who bought a house, and it was her first client she sold a house to, so it was definitely a win for the both of us. There is power in connecting with people who are on their path to greatness. You will find the power of two when you realize that everything you need is not always within you. There are people on your path who are designed to help you, but they can't help you until you are willing to help them.

I was glad I was able to pay it forward and help her get her career started like she helped me back in the day. On your road to greatness, it will be full of fresh starts, but there are people on your path who are waiting for you, and you are waiting for them.

BET ON YOU

You are your most valuable asset. You may not realize it quite yet, but you will soon find the value in yourself and allow yourself to be yourself.

Once you learn to value yourself, you will see everything you need on your path. Until you value the greatness within you, you will bet on everyone else.

To bet on yourself, believe in yourself, and trust yourself are the greatest gifts that you can give to yourself. From there, you will find yourself betting on others only because you see yourself in them and them in you.

Life is full of twists and turns, and the dirty parts are cleaner than you think. When you position yourself for growth and change, you will learn the lessons along the way.

Everything you need is within you, but you must bet on yourself in order to win. Once you see yourself winning more than losing, you will see that you were destined to win.

Until the next time...

Derrick Anthony Pickett

CONTACT US

For more information on starting your journey towards changing your life through credit restoration, please feel free to contact our office. If you would like for me to speak to your civic, religious, or business group, please feel free to contact me directly.

Total Source Consulting Service
450 South Orange Ave
3rd Floor
Orlando, FL 32801

Derrick Pickett
The Credit Guru
678-592-1624
thecreditguru@icloud.com
derrickpickett.com

DΞRRICK PICKΞTT

Made in the USA
Columbia, SC
13 November 2020